THE LITTLE BOOK OF
ASTROLOGY

JUDITH HURRELL

summersdale

THE LITTLE BOOK OF ASTROLOGY

An Hachette UK Company
www.hachette.co.uk

Summersdale Publishers
Part of Octopus Publishing Group Limited
Carmelite House
50 Victoria Embankment
LONDON
EC4Y 0DZ
UK

www.summersdale.com

Printed and bound in Poland

ISBN: 978-1-83799-392-5

This FSC® label means that materials used for the product have been responsibly sourced

MIX
Paper | Supporting responsible forestry
FSC® C018236

Substantial discounts on bulk quantities of Summersdale books are available to corporations, professional associations and other organizations. For details contact general enquiries: telephone: +44 (0) 1243 771107 or email: enquiries@summersdale.com.

CONTENTS

★ INTRODUCTION ★

Do you love reading your horoscope? When you meet someone new, do you find yourself asking, "What's your star sign?" Do you thank your lucky stars when things go your way or blame hitches and delays on Mercury in retrograde?

If so, you're already tuned into astrology! *The Little Book of Astrology* will ignite this curiosity, bringing even more inspiration, guidance and understanding to light.

The word astrology comes from the Greek words *astron*, meaning "star" and *logos*, meaning "word" or "reason". As such, astrology can be defined as the study of stars and their perceived influence on human affairs and natural events.

The appeal of astrology is timeless. People from all cultures have appreciated the stars' glow and looked to them for meaning since the earliest human civilizations.

Such a vast history means the subject can feel as infinite and mysterious as the universe itself. But fear not; with this beginner's guide, all will become clear. Read on to shine a light on exciting paths ahead, channel the wisdom of the heavens and transcend the limits of your earthly existence. It's time to go stellar!

CHAPTER ONE:
WHAT IS ASTROLOGY?

Astrology is an ancient belief system that many feel holds the key to harnessing the power of the stars in your life. But to decode the secrets of this ancient belief system, first, you must understand its foundations.

There's no need to feel daunted. For millennia, all types of people from all over the world have embraced astrology. While the practice has evolved, its core principles remain the same, with many systems sharing similar beliefs and tools.

This chapter explores the cornerstones at the heart of astrology, including its rhythmical systems, guiding principles and exciting practical applications. Understand these and you, too, can harness the wisdom and knowledge of the universe.

THE HISTORY AND EVOLUTION OF ASTROLOGY

Humankind has been seeking meaning in the skies since the earliest civilizations. Archaeologists have found dots corresponding to celestial bodies in the Stone Age cave art of Lascaux, France and Aboriginal Australian rock art from 40,000 to 60,000 years ago.

Similarly, archaeological evidence suggests the ancestral Puebloan peoples of Chaco Canyon, New Mexico, may have captured lunar and solar movements in their prehistoric rock carvings. Likewise, the art of Painted Rock in California, estimated to be thousands of years old, aligns with the solstices. These artworks offer intriguing glimpses into how our ancestors may have connected and interacted with the cosmos.

The earliest known astrological system began in ancient Mesopotamia around the third millennium BCE. Babylonian astronomers carved astrological records onto clay tablets, predating the construction of the Great Pyramid of Giza in Egypt and Stonehenge in Britain.

Vedic astrology, or Jyotish, originated in India around 1500 BCE or earlier. The practice was based on the Vedas – ancient scriptures written over several centuries in ancient India. The Rigveda, one of the oldest Vedic sources, dates back around 3,000 to 4,000 years. Therefore, Vedic astrology reflects the popular concepts of that time, such as karma and reincarnation.

Astrology also thrived in ancient Greece. In the second century CE, Claudius Ptolemy, a famous astrologer of the Greco-Roman era, wrote a book called the *Almagest*, exploring the movements of celestial bodies.

Records suggest that early Chinese astronomers during the Warring States period (475–221 BCE) observed Jupiter's approximate 12-year orbit, naming Jupiter the "Year Star" (*Suixing*). However, the foundation of the zodiac system likely emerged during the Western Han Dynasty (206 BCE–9 CE), drawing on the lunar calendar and ancient Chinese philosophy.

During the Islamic Golden Age, between the eighth and fourteenth centuries CE, Arab and Persian scholars created their own astrological traditions by translating texts from Greek and Babylonian cultures into Arabic – safekeeping and sharing valuable ancient knowledge.

During the medieval period, this ripple of Arabic translations spread astrological knowledge to Europe. Translations of Greek and Babylonian ideas from Arabic into Latin from the twelfth century onwards went on to shape European astrology.

Great European thinkers like Pico della Mirandola, Marsilio Ficino and Johannes Kepler were deeply moved by Greek and Babylonian ideas, inspiring a new astrological landscape in medieval and Renaissance Europe.

During the late nineteenth century, Western astrology integrated many ancient principles. Today, contemporary astrologers blend tradition with modern insights and adapt the subject to diverse perspectives.

With the help of technology, contemporary astrology is becoming more accessible and accepted. As the exploration continues, it enriches our understanding of the universe and the human experience, providing a profound wisdom that transcends time and space.

SOCIALLY
★ CONSCIOUS ASTROLOGY ★

At its heart, astrology is the art of linking celestial phenomena to human experiences and behaviour. But of course, everyone's life experience is unique, as is their resulting behaviour.

This truth explains why astrology has been practised in myriad ways across cultures and history, evolving into distinct traditions with unique characteristics.

No matter how you develop and express your interest in astrology, it's vital to approach these traditions in culturally sensitive, inclusive and ethical ways, avoiding stereotypes, cultural appropriations or biases.

Some astrological practices involve cultural symbols or customs: you should understand and respect their cultural context before using them. Likewise, to avoid perpetuating stereotypes, it's important to be mindful of the language used in traditional texts – for example, the association of certain qualities with masculine or feminine energies.

Luckily, all astrological systems share a belief in the connection between celestial patterns and earthly events – making them universal and open to everyone.

★ THE SYSTEMS OF ASTROLOGY ★

Did you know there are many astrological systems, all with a unique appeal? Each one prioritizes celestial elements slightly differently based on their cultural, historical and philosophical origins. If that feels like a lot to get your head around, don't worry. All systems share similar basic principles, weaving in common trusted threads.

Western astrology focuses on specific zodiac signs and their influence on personality traits and life events. This system places great importance on the sun, moon and planets visible in our solar system. The sun represents an individual's identity, whereas the moon reflects emotions and instincts.

Similarly, **Vedic astrology** also focuses on the positions of celestial bodies, including the sun, moon and planets. Again, the moon is highly revered for its impact on mental and emotional well-being.

Also known as **Kabbalistic astrology**, **Jewish astrology** integrates mystical and spiritual aspects of Judaism. It combines interpretations of the Hebrew calendar, the positions of celestial bodies and their influence on Jewish traditions and spirituality.

In contrast, **Native American astrology** sees cosmic events as part of nature, which can be harnessed for healing, prayer and communicating with the spiritual realm. Seasonal rituals and ceremonies often draw on celestial events, such as lunar phases or meteor showers and the energy they bring to particular times of the year.

Chinese astrology follows a 12-year zodiac cycle where each year corresponds to an animal sign. These signs and the five elements influence an individual's personality, behaviour and future. In contrast to other systems, stars and planets play a minimal role.

No matter what strand or blend of astrology you feel drawn to, it offers a unique lens to explore your personal growth, relationships, destiny and place in the universe. Chapter Two will help you explore these systems in more depth.

★ WHAT ASTROLOGY ★ CAN DO FOR YOU

Suppose you need a personal event planner, a **GPS** to guide you through life, or a matchmaker to enhance your relationships. Astrology fills all these roles and more thanks to its many techniques and applications.

Synastry astrology is where Cupid's arrow meets astral coordinates to reveal the planets' influence on relationships. It's a cosmic matchmaker, helping us understand compatibility and relationship dynamics for harmonious connections.

Electional astrology helps choose the best times for important events by aligning actions with celestial energies – let the stars guide you to the perfect day to tie the knot or launch your business.

Locational astrology is like a cosmic GPS, using planetary influences to guide you to the ideal locations for significant life events, from career changes to holiday romance. So, you may like to consult your astrological compass before you put down roots or quench your wanderlust!

Need to phone a friend about a burning question? **Horary astrology** is a divinatory art that uses chart analysis to answer specific questions at the moment of enquiry – your hotline to a heavenly help desk.

Taking its name from the Latin word *mundus*, meaning "world" or "universe", **Mundane astrology** extends its gaze beyond individual concerns towards global affairs and world events, revealing celestial patterns that pulse throughout humanity.

Psychological astrology illuminates individual concerns and invites us to explore the depths of the psyche. Think of it as a cosmic therapist who decodes the planets' imprints on our personalities, relationships and life paths.

Imagine these branches of astrology as your personal support squad: synastry, your cosmic matchmaker; electional, your diary planner; locational, your cosmic compass; horary, your insightful decision maker; mundane, your worldly advisor; and psychological, your celestial therapist. It's like the whole universe is at your service.

★ ASTROLOGY FOR ★ RELATIONSHIPS

Want to understand your relationships better? An astrological toolkit can help you decipher friendship dynamics, office politics or cosmic compatibility with a new partner.

Astrology has always been a tool for understanding relationships. Western astrology uses synastry to compare natal charts for relationship insights. Chinese astrology uses the zodiac's animal signs to determine compatibility. Vedic astrology's "Kuta Milan" evaluates partners' moon signs and stars for affinity. Kabbalah looks at divine structure to interpret relationships in the context of spiritual paths.

But even if you're new to astrology, online platforms and astrology apps make generating and comparing natal charts for compatibility a breeze, so insights are only ever a click away.

Even without a birth chart, knowing someone's sun sign – otherwise known as a zodiac or star sign – is insightful. This sign provides a broad understanding of communication styles, love languages and compatibility.

ASTROLOGY FOR
⋆ WELLNESS AND FULFILMENT ⋆

Astrology can also offer profound insights into the foundations and fluctuations of your health, mood, direction, purpose and place in the world, supercharging your well-being.

Western astrology uses personalized horoscopes for self-awareness and decision-making. Chinese astrology employs the zodiac for life guidance. Vedic astrology uses gemstones and mantras to counteract planetary negatives and boost overall well-being. Native American cultures draw on celestial observations to inform their rituals, ceremonies and medicinal practices to align individual and collective well-being with astrological rhythms.

Exploring your birth chart is a way to reflect on your emotional needs, planetary influences and harmonious or challenging energies. Observing astrological events can encourage present moment awareness, mindfulness and a sense of connection to something greater than yourself.

Thus, astrology provides a holistic path to wellness that aligns with cosmic rhythms for a more fulfilling life journey.

★ ASTROLOGY FOR ★ CONTEMPLATION

Have you ever marvelled at the vastness of the night sky or felt awed by a shooting star? If so, you'll understand why astrology has always been intertwined with contemplation.

Astrology inspires wonder, asking us to examine our place in the universe. Historically, various cultures have attributed divine significance to planets, constellations and celestial events based on mythology, religion and tradition.

Ancient cultures worshipped the sun and moon as representations of vitality and the ebb and flow of life. In Roman mythology, Jupiter was the king of gods, while Polaris symbolized guidance and constancy. Egyptians observed that Orion set in the west, the direction they associated with death and the afterlife. Hence, Orion became linked with Osiris, the god of the underworld and rebirth.

Modern astrology welcomes any connection with deities but does not require it. Whether during ceremony, ritual or a casual glance at the heavens, connecting with the universal mystery is all that matters.

★ THE ZODIAC ★

The zodiac is at the heart of Western astrology. It's a celestial sphere divided into 12 sections linked to specific constellations.

These sections, known as astrological signs, correspond to the path of the sun across roughly 30 degrees of the sky throughout the year.

Aries: 21 March–19 April
Taurus: 20 April–20 May
Gemini: 21 May–20 June
Cancer: 21 June–22 July
Leo: 23 July–22 August
Virgo: 23 August–22 September
Libra: 23 September–22 October
Scorpio: 23 October–21 November
Sagittarius: 22 November–21 December
Capricorn: 22 December–19 January
Aquarius: 20 January–18 February
Pisces: 19 February–20 March

The position of the sun at your time of birth determines your zodiac sign.

★ THE NATAL CHART ★

Discovering your natal chart is an exciting step on your astrological journey.

This chart is a cosmic snapshot of the sky at the time of your birth, showing the positions of celestial bodies relative to the Earth.

The chart is divided into 12 houses, each representing different areas of your life. Planets and celestial bodies, including the sun and moon, are placed within these houses to illustrate their positions at the moment of your birth. Their positions offer insights into your personality, relationships and life path. Your zodiac sign further colours these planetary influences, with each sign being associated with one of four elements: fire, earth, air and water.

Astrologers analyze the angles or aspects between planets to offer increasingly nuanced interpretations. Beginners often start exploring their sun, moon and rising signs. These vital features influence core identity, emotional nature and outer demeanour.

As you journey deeper into astrology, the map of your natal chart will unfurl further, guiding you closer to self-discovery and an understanding of life's patterns.

⭑ PLANETARY INFLUENCES ⭑

In astrology, each planet symbolizes distinct qualities and governs specific aspects of life, shaping an individual's traits and experiences.

★ The sun represents your core identity and ego, influencing self-expression and vitality.

★ The moon reflects emotions, intuition and the subconscious, shaping your emotional responses and nurturing instincts.

★ Mercury governs communication, intellect and adaptability, influencing your thought processes and social interactions.

★ Venus rules love, relationships and aesthetics, impacting your approach to beauty, pleasure and emotional ties.

★ Mars symbolizes energy, drive and assertiveness, influencing ambition, passion and how you pursue goals.

★ Jupiter expands horizons, symbolizing growth, abundance and optimism, shaping your approach to opportunities and wealth.

★ Saturn represents discipline, responsibility and structure, influencing long-term goals, challenges and life lessons.

★ RISING SIGNS ★

Your rising sign, or ascendant, is a crucial part of your natal chart. It's the constellation that was rising on the eastern horizon at your time of birth.

All 12 zodiac signs pass through the ascendant over the course of a day, each spending around two hours in this position.

This is why astrologists are so particular about knowing your exact time of birth. Even twins born just a few moments apart could have different rising signs, making their birth charts quite different.

Your rising sign reveals the persona you present to the world. Think of it like a cosmic filter, influencing how the world perceives you. It's the mask you wear when you arrive at a party, stand up to make a speech or introduce yourself for the first time.

Your rising sign may be more relatable to you than your sun sign, as the traits associated with it are often those you value. This persona is a prominent aspect of your identity, embodying the characteristics you apply in social settings – your astrological "game face" in the sport of life.

✦ ASPECTS ✦

The angles formed between planets on your birth chart are called aspects. The main aspects include conjunctions, sextiles, squares, trines and oppositions, each revealing a unique interplay of energies between celestial bodies.

★ Conjunctions happen when two celestial bodies are within approximately 0 to 10 degrees of each other. This position intensifies and magnifies their energies.

★ A sextile is a harmonious aspect when two planets are 60 degrees apart, bringing opportunities, creativity and positive interactions between the planets involved.

★ Squares occur when two celestial bodies are 90 degrees apart. This aspect brings up tension, conflict and growth opportunities.

★ A trine is a harmonious aspect occurring when two celestial bodies are 120 degrees apart. It brings positive energy, natural talent, ease and cooperation between the planets.

★ When two celestial bodies are 180 degrees apart, they are said to be in opposition. This aspect creates tension, polarization and a need for balance and integration.

✦ ASTROLOGICAL HOUSES ✦

As you learned earlier, the 360-degree circle of your natal chart contains 12 houses. These houses are associated with particular zodiac signs and provide a framework for understanding your life experience.

Each house represents a different area of your life, covering everything from identity, finances, possessions, values, communications, family relationships, journeys, creativity, health, work, partnerships and enemies to resources, change, education, travel, philosophy, friendships, public life, subconscious, spirituality and hidden influences.

To interpret a natal chart, astrologers look at the zodiac sign on the cusp of each house and any planets within it at your time of birth. They also look at the ruling planet for the zodiac sign on the cusp of each house for additional information. These details provide insights into your journey, motivations and potential life path.

Understanding the intricate dynamics and subtle connections in celestial arrangements can be complicated and true understanding is a lifetime's work. Chapter Three provides an introduction. Approaching with practice, curiosity and an open mind is enough!

★ TRANSITS AND PROGRESSIONS ★

Transits and progressions are dynamic tools in astrology, illuminating the ever-changing cosmic influences on an individual's life.

Transits refer to the current positions of planets as they interact with their positions in your natal chart. These momentary alignments provide insights into short-term trends influencing emotions, relationships and opportunities. By observing transits, you can better understand the unfolding narrative of your life.

Progressions look at the development of the natal chart over a longer period. Techniques like secondary progressions advance the positions of planets in the chart at a symbolic rate, often reflecting internal growth and shifting life perspectives. Progressions offer a more gradual, long-term view, revealing the journey of your soul and its developmental arcs.

By integrating transits and progressions, astrologers can gain a comprehensive understanding of the challenges, growth opportunities and pivotal life events that lie ahead. Together, these tools weave a dynamic astrological tapestry, guiding you through the evolving chapters of your life.

✦ ELEMENTS AND MODALITIES ✦

Astrology uses elements and modalities to categorize zodiac signs, enabling you to explore your sign holistically.

The Elements: fire, earth, air and water represent the fundamental qualities associated with each group of signs.

- ★ Fire Signs (Aries, Leo, Sagittarius) manifest enthusiasm, passion and inspiration.
- ★ Earth Signs (Taurus, Virgo, Capricorn) embody practicality, stability and groundedness.
- ★ Air Signs (Gemini, Libra, Aquarius) personify intellectualism, communication and focus.
- ★ Water Signs (Cancer, Scorpio, Pisces) epitomize emotion, intuition and sensitivity.

The Modalities: cardinal, fixed and mutable indicate a sign's dynamic or action-oriented qualities.

- ★ Cardinal Signs (Aries, Cancer, Libra, Capricorn) are initiators and catalysts for action, inspiring change.
- ★ Fixed Signs (Taurus, Leo, Scorpio, Aquarius) maintain the status quo, providing persistence and determination.
- ★ Mutable Signs (Gemini, Virgo, Sagittarius, Pisces) adapt to change, representing flexibility and transition.

✦ DEEPENING YOUR KNOWLEDGE ✦

This first chapter includes an abundance of information to kindle your curiosity about astrology. The following chapters take a deep dive into astrological systems and history, allowing you to immerse yourself in your new passion. It's never been easier to take your astrological learning off the page into the big wide world!

Join online astrology communities: Learn, connect and share ideas with astrology enthusiasts all over the world.

Source a personalized birth chart: Free online tools can help you unveil a map of the planets and constellations at your time of birth.

Astrology apps: Having daily forecasts and bitesize astrology content at your fingertips – what's not to love?

Planetary podcasts: Listen to engaging discussions and practical tips for interpreting your chart and the latest planetary movements.

Remember, the journey is just as important as the destination. Open your mind, connect with your tribe, embrace the unknown and let the stars illuminate your path!

CHAPTER TWO:
TYPES OF
ASTROLOGY

Just as the night sky looks different from different corners of Earth, so too does astrology. Chapter Two invites you to peer into a cosmic kaleidoscope. Every twist of the lens unveils a different astrological tradition, taking in Chinese, Vedic, Hindu, Jewish, Native American and Modern Western viewpoints.

In this cosmic adventure, you'll explore the diverse landscapes of astrology and its rich cultural and historical roots. This holistic understanding will enable you to reach far and wide for astrological insights, fostering a panoramic connection with the cosmos.

Understanding various astrological practices will also expand your awareness of other belief systems and cultures. It will foster empathy and appreciation for diverse perspectives on how cosmic energies may influence your life.

Ultimately, embracing the richness of various astrological traditions will empower you with the knowledge and grounding for a more profound connection with other astrology enthusiasts and the universe.

★ CHINESE ASTROLOGY ★

The rich and ancient history of Chinese astrology dates back to the early dynastic periods in China. Its roots are deeply ingrained in the philosophical and cultural traditions of the country. They can be traced to the ancient practices of divination and cosmology prevalent during the Shang Dynasty (c. 1600–1046 BCE) and the Zhou Dynasty (1046–256 BCE) when early astrologists began tying their observations of celestial bodies to earthly events.

In the sixth century BCE, Confucianism significantly influenced the development of Chinese astrology. Confucianism, founded by the philosopher Confucius, emphasized ethical conduct, social harmony and the proper functioning of societal structures. These principles contributed to the idea that celestial patterns and their interpretation could guide rulers in maintaining a just and harmonious society.

Taoism began to influence Chinese astrology during the early periods of the Zhou Dynasty, which spanned from the eleventh century BCE to 256 BCE.

Its fundamental text, the *Dao De Jing* - attributed to the thinker Laozi - was pivotal in shaping Chinese astrological beliefs. Taoism emphasizes the natural order of the universe and the interconnectedness of all things. The belief in cycles and the balance of yin and yang became crucial in understanding the rhythms and repeating patterns of the cosmos seen in Chinese astrology.

Chinese astrology has evolved with the help of several historical figures and events. Huangdi, also known as the Yellow Emperor, is a legendary figure in Chinese mythology and is credited with organizing and systematizing early astrological knowledge. During the Han Dynasty (206 BCE–220 CE), the Chinese zodiac, with its 12 animal signs and associated earthly branches, was developed and integrated deeply into Chinese culture. Since then, this system has influenced astrological beliefs, art, literature and daily life in China.

★ CHINESE ASTROLOGY ★ MYTHS AND LEGENDS

According to ancient Chinese mythology, the Chinese zodiac originated from a legendary race organized by the Jade Emperor. The emperor wanted to establish an order for the zodiac signs, so he invited animals to a race. The clever rat knew he had no chance, so he hitched a ride on the back of the diligent ox. The rat swiftly jumped off as they approached the finish line, claiming the inaugural spot. The hardworking ox earned second place, with the resourceful tiger, compassionate rabbit and majestic dragon following suit based on their traits.

There's always been speculation about a cat, known for its agility, did not participate in the race. Some legends claim the cat missed the race due to the rat's trickery, etching their rivalry in celestial lore.

These legends reveal that astrology was more than a divination tool for the ancient Chinese. It was imbued with wisdom and moral teachings to emphasize the importance of harmony and interdependence within the grand cosmic order.

⭐ THE WINNING ATTRIBUTES ⭐ OF THE 12 SIGNS

So, who were the lucky 12? The lineup included a rat, an ox, a tiger, a rabbit, a dragon, a snake, a horse, a goat (or sheep), a monkey, a rooster, a dog and a pig.

Each animal in the cosmic menagerie possesses a unique attribute that is symbolic rather than hierarchical in nature.

Hence, those born in the Year of the Rat are seen as intelligent, while those born in the Year of the Ox are considered diligent. Tigers are known for their boldness and Rabbits are thought to be compassionate. Dragons are majestic and people born in the Year of the Snake are believed to have wisdom. Horses are known for their free-spirited energy and Goats for their gentleness. Monkeys are playful, Roosters are enthusiastic and Dogs are loyal. People born in the Year of the Pig are considered sincere.

★ THE EARTHLY BRANCHES ★ AND HEAVENLY STEMS

The Earthly Branches and Heavenly Stems are important parts of an ancient 60-year cyclical system that is fundamental to traditional Chinese cosmology, astrology and timekeeping. Each year in the cycle has a unique pairing of Heavenly Stems and Earthly Branches, which helps to understand time, seasons and cosmic influences.

Heavenly Stems (Tian Gan):

The Heavenly Stems are ten characters representing five elements and a yin or yang polarity.

Jia (甲) – Yang Wood
Yi (乙) – Yin Wood
Bing (丙) – Yang Fire
Ding (丁) – Yin Fire
Wu (戊) – Yang Earth
Ji (己) – Yin Earth
Geng (庚) – Yang Metal
Xin (辛) – Yin Metal
Ren (壬) – Yang Water
Gui (癸) – Yin Water

Earthly Branches (Di Zhi):

The Earthly Branches are associated with a specific month, direction and season, as well as 12 animal characters from the Chinese zodiac.

1. Zi (Rat)

2. Chou (Ox)

3. Yin (Tiger)

4. Mao (Rabbit)

5. Chen (Dragon)

6. Si (Snake)

7. Wu (Horse)

8. Wei (Goat)

9. Shen (Monkey)

10. You (Rooster)

11. Xu (Dog)

12. Hai (Pig)

★ THE FOUR PILLARS OF DESTINY ★

The Four Pillars of Destiny, or Ba Zi, is a Chinese astrological system based on a person's year, month, day and hour of birth. This information is analyzed alongside an Earthly Stem and Heavenly Branch pairing to reveal a set of eight characters.

Astrologers analyze:

1. The Heavenly Stem and Earthly Branch associated with a person's birth year.

2. The Heavenly Stem and Earthly Branch related to a person's birth month.

3. The Heavenly Stem and Earthly Branch associated with a person's birth day.

4. The Heavenly Stem and Earthly Branch related to a person's birth hour.

These eight characters help Chinese astrologers understand a person's personality, strengths, weaknesses and possible life paths.

It's a holistic approach that forms the foundation of many Chinese calendars and divination systems.

✦ CHINESE ASTROLOGY TODAY ✦

If you've ever celebrated Chinese New Year, you'll know Chinese astrology still influences popular cultural traditions. The zodiac animal of each year is celebrated and honoured during festivities.

People often follow certain customs and practices based on their zodiac sign to attract good fortune and maintain balance. Chinese astrology is integral to celebrations, where individuals offer prayers, light fireworks and share symbolic foods.

Observing your Ben Ming Nian, or Year of Birth, is another traditional practice that links to the Chinese zodiac. This tradition occurs every 12 years when someone's zodiac sign matches the sign of the current year.

According to Chinese astrology, individuals may face obstacles or transformations at this time. To ward off bad luck, people often wear red to symbolize good fortune and protection, follow Feng Shui principles or take part in rituals.

These customs reflect the influence of the zodiac on daily life in modern China, emphasizing the importance of considering astrological forces for a more harmonious existence.

★ HISTORY OF VEDIC ASTROLOGY ★

Vedic astrology, also known as Jyotish, has a rich and ancient history dating back thousands of years. It encompasses diverse schools and traditions, each with unique interpretations and techniques and an emphasis on astrological principles and applications.

Vedic astrology evolved from the Vedas – the sacred texts of India – to become a systematic study of celestial influences on human life.

Early Vedic scholars studied celestial movements to understand cosmic forces and their impact on people. Integrating Persian and Greek astrological concepts enriched the tradition during the Hellenistic era from the fourth century BCE. During the Gupta period in the sixth century CE, Vedic astrology flourished, with notable astrologer Varāhamihira authoring a renowned work called the *Brihat Jataka* (Great Birth Chart).

With the availability of Vedic texts and increased global interest, modern Vedic astrology has transcended cultural boundaries. Renowned astrologers like B. V. Raman and current practitioners have earned international recognition.

Today, Vedic astrology thrives as a respected discipline, offering insights into human life, spirituality and karma.

✦ THE VEDIC NATAL CHART ✦

At the heart of Vedic astrology is the Janam Kundali, a cosmic blueprint at the moment of a person's birth. This birth chart captures an intricate map of the planets within specific zodiac signs and houses.

Astrologers can zoom in and out of the Janam Kundali to take panoramic perspectives and intricate close-ups of a person's astrological disposition. They look at:

★ **Main 12 houses:** these give a feel for the broader aspects of a person's life, such as self, family, career and spirituality.
★ **Specialized divisional charts:** these give more detailed insights and nuanced perspectives into specific life areas, such as marriage and career.
★ **Nakshatras or "lunar mansions":** these divide the zodiac into 27 constellations, each associated with unique qualities, attributes and ruling deities.
★ **Planetary aspects and transits:** these look at the interaction of planets in the Janam Kundali and their movement over time, influencing the Nakshatras, houses and specialized divisional charts.

★ PLANETARY INFLUENCES ★

The nine planets, or grahas, have a starring role in Vedic astrology. They each have distinct characteristics with the power to add shape and nuance to an individual's life.

★ The sun governs an individual's vitality and influences their core identity.
★ The moon represents emotions and intuition.
★ Mars brings energy, courage and determination.
★ Mercury, the communicator, affects intelligence and communication skills.
★ Jupiter symbolizes wisdom, benevolence and prosperity.
★ Venus governs love, beauty and creativity.
★ Saturn, the taskmaster, influences discipline and life lessons.
★ Rahu and Ketu, known as the lunar nodes, add karmic dimensions to the chart.

The position of each planet in specific houses and signs during an individual's birth creates their unique cosmic DNA. The influences of each planet can be either beneficial or challenging, depending on a person's character and the position of the planets in relation to each other.

★ YOGAS AND DOSHAS ★

In Vedic astrology, the term yoga refers to the arrangement of planets in a person's birth chart. Yogas can be either auspicious or inauspicious, revealing an individual's potential in specific areas, such as personality, career or relationships. For instance, Raj yoga suggests prosperity and authority, while Kemadruma yoga points towards challenges and difficulties.

Doshas are negative influences caused by the unfavourable placement of certain planets in a birth chart. The primary doshas are Kaal Sarpa dosha, indicating challenges and obstacles and Mangal dosha, associated with marital discord.

But don't worry! Astrologers who understand yogas and doshas can remedy harmful planetary combinations. They provide targeted advice and remedies to limit potential hardships. In this proactive way, Vedic astrology helps individuals navigate life's challenges and optimize their potential for success and fulfilment.

★ KARMA AND VEDIC ASTROLOGY ★

Have you heard of karma? If you've used the phrase "what goes around comes around" or "you reap what you sow", you may be familiar with the concept.

The word means "action" and sums up the idea that individual actions shape destiny, creating a cycle of consequences.

But did you know that karma is deeply entwined with Vedic astrology? According to Vedic astrology, a person's natal chart, or horoscope, is a reflection of their accumulated karma from past lives. If this concept sounds deterministic, you'll be relieved that there's also plenty of room for free will and conscious choice.

Vedic astrology tells us that restorative actions and ethical living can downgrade the impact of challenging planetary arrangements, creating spiritual growth and positive experiences. People can use tools like mantra chanting, acts of charity and gemstones to balance their karma.

This emphasis on conscious, mindful life choices, self-awareness and a sense of responsibility is one reason Vedic astrology is so helpful today.

★ REMEDIES AND RITUALS ★ IN VEDIC ASTROLOGY

Vedic astrology uses rituals and remedies to harness cosmic powers and enhance well-being, such as:

★ Financial issues caused by afflictions to the second house or planet Jupiter are treated by chanting the Jupiter mantra "Om Guruve Namaha" and wearing yellow sapphire or citrine.

★ Relationship problems caused by afflictions to the seventh house or Venus are treated by chanting the Venus mantra "Om Shukraya Namaha" and wearing a diamond or white sapphire.

★ Career obstacles caused by malefic aspects in the tenth house or afflictions to the sun are treated by chanting the sun mantra "Om Suryaya Namaha" and wearing a ruby or coral.

★ Poor health related to the sixth house or malefic aspects on the moon are treated by reciting the moon mantra "Om Somaya Namaha" and wearing a pearl.

★ Communication problems due to afflictions to the third house, Mercury, are treated by reciting the Mercury mantra "Om Budhaya Namaha" and wearing an emerald.

★ MODERN APPLICATIONS ★ OF VEDIC ASTROLOGY

In the self-care era, Vedic astrology is more relevant than ever. No matter where you are on your astrology journey, calling in the cosmos and crafting rituals for self-improvement will bring a new dimension to your wellness.

When it comes to relationships, Vedic astrology can offer insights into your compatibility with a partner, potential challenges and advice on improving harmony by examining your seventh house.

Delving into your tenth house will throw light on your professional strengths and weaknesses, helping you make well-informed career choices. Looking at planetary positions can illuminate career paths and an awareness of unfavourable planetary alignments can help you avoid pitfalls.

For health matters, Vedic astrology analyzes the first house and the influence of planets on the ascendant. Understanding potential weaknesses can help you to take a nurturing, preventive approach.

Despite its ancient roots, these modern-day applications show why Vedic astrology has never been more current!

THE HISTORY OF ASTROLOGY IN JUDAISM

Let's untangle the long history of celestial fascination in Judaism and the complicated crossovers of astrology and Jewish beliefs. Jewish scholars were first introduced to the practice of astrology during ancient times through interactions with neighbouring Babylonian and Persian cultures. This led to discussions about the merits and limitations of astrology, which were documented in Talmudic literature from the second to the fifth century CE.

During medieval times, Jewish scholars such as Abraham Ibn Ezra (c. 1089–1167) studied astrological literature in Arabic and Latin, adding to the debate. Ibn Ezra was a prominent Spanish-Jewish scholar, poet, philosopher, commentator on the Hebrew Bible and astrologer. He combined the Hebrew religious, philosophical and cultural practices with Greco-Arabic astrological knowledge, writing several influential texts. His writings integrated astronomy, astrology and Jewish thought and explained the astrological impacts on human destiny.

The Kabbalistic tradition flourished in the twelfth and thirteenth centuries, offering mystical insights into Judaism. The Zohar, a significant text in the Kabbalistic tradition, introduced symbolic connections between celestial bodies and divine attributes. Kabbalists believe these connections represent hidden spiritual forces underlying the physical world.

During the Renaissance era, Jewish scholars became interested in studying astrology. However, they faced a dilemma in reconciling the influence of celestial bodies with Jewish principles of divine providence and the concept of free will.

Nowadays, some Jewish communities, especially those interested in mysticism or New Age spirituality, still use astrological insights for their personal growth and spiritual development. However, mainstream Judaism approaches astrology cautiously as it is viewed as a form of divination that could potentially lead to idolatry.

This complex relationship explains why astrology is still a hotly debated topic within various strands of the Jewish community.

CONTEMPORARY
★ PERSPECTIVES ★
AND TECHNIQUES

The relationship between astrology and Judaism remains intricate and complex. While mainstream Judaism has discouraged it, some individuals use astrology for self-reflection and spiritual insight.

Kabbalah, an esoteric branch of Judaism, has recently experienced a revival. This trend reflects a growing interest in the mystical elements of Judaism in today's diverse and changing society.

The Zohar is a Kabbalistic book that uses astrology to explain spiritual principles. According to the book, planetary alignment reflects divine energies on Earth.

The Zohar draws a connection between astrology and spirituality. Kabbalists compare God's ten attributes or emanations, known as *sefirot*, to the zodiac signs. Planetary movements are seen as sources of spiritual energy. They encourage their followers to look for divine messages and spiritual truths within the cosmic sphere.

Kabbalistic astrology is a means of understanding the interconnectedness of the cosmos and the divine. Key principles include:

★ The symbolic Tree of Life that links branches to celestial bodies.
★ Planetary positions relative to astrological signs that shape personal transformation.
★ Gematria, which assigns numerical values to Hebrew letters for deeper understanding.
★ Tikkun, which involves aligning or repairing the soul's connection to the divine.
★ Meditative practices to aid in attuning to spiritual energies.

This mystical system provides a holistic approach to self-enquiry and transformation, attracting spiritual seekers with and without religious faith.

Likewise, many contemporary Jewish people engage with other strands of astrology through a lens of personal growth and introspection, blending ancient wisdom with a modern quest for self-discovery.

★ ASTROLOGY IN NATIVE ★ AMERICAN TRADITIONS

Astrology has had deep roots in Native American culture since ancient times. Rather than being a stand-alone practice, the deep connection many of these tribes feel with the cosmos is woven into the fabric of their spiritual traditions, daily life and sacred rituals.

Astrological connections are expressed uniquely within tribes, reflecting the distinctiveness of their history, environment and beliefs. For instance, the Lakota people from the Great Plains believe that the position of the stars and planets can help predict future events, while the Hopi people from the south-west associate different constellations with specific seasons and natural phenomena. The Navajo tribe, also in the south-west, believe celestial positions hold messages about balance in physical and spiritual realms. They worship the stars, moon and sun and rely on them to guide agricultural decisions.

Across all these traditions, astrology remains an essential aspect of Native American ritual, connecting the tribes to their ancestors and the natural world.

NATIVE AMERICAN
★ ASTROLOGICAL RITUALS ★
AND CEREMONIES

Night Chant Ceremony

The Night Chant ceremony, or Yébîchai ceremony, holds astrological significance among the Navajo people. The festivities last nine nights and involve intricate sand painting and ceremonial dances. The festival goers use these to seek blessings of health and prosperity. Skilled astronomers in the tribe time the ceremony to coincide with astronomical events such as the appearance of the Pleiades.

Sundance Rituals

For the Lakota Sioux, the sun symbolizes life and energy. During the summer solstice they perform Sundance ceremonies. Participants fast and dance around a sacred tree, seeking spiritual renewal. The ceremony connects participants with cosmic forces, fostering healing, vision quests and communal solidarity within the Lakota community.

Solstice and Equinox Rituals

The Zuni tribe celebrate their complex cosmology on the solstices and equinoxes. During these rituals, the Zuni pay homage to the sun and its influence on agriculture and spiritual welfare. The Zuni intentionally orientate their sacred sites to capture the light of the rising and setting sun and align their festivals to celestial cycles.

Skywatching for Lunar Guidance

The Mohawk Nation draw lunar observations into their spiritual practices. Skywatching elders pay close attention to the moon's phases to pinpoint the ideal timing for ceremonies, agricultural activities and communal gatherings. The moon is seen as a celestial guide, influencing practical aspects of life and offering spiritual insights through its changing face.

Star Knowledge in Vision Quests

The Blackfeet Confederacy weave their intimate knowledge of the stars into their vision quests. Individuals align their quests with specific constellations to seek guidance and purpose, emphasizing their connection between personal introspection and cosmic forces.

★ ASTROLOGICAL SYMBOLISM ★

Within Native American cultures, celestial bodies often bear profound symbolism, each holding unique significance. It's essential to recognize that there are diverse beliefs within tribes and that interpretations of celestial phenomena may differ.

The Sun
The sun is vital for existence, symbolizing life, warmth and growth. Its daily and seasonal journey has historically shaped the rhythm of life in many Native American cultures. Its masculine energy is associated with life and seasonal changes.

The Moon
For centuries, the moon has been a symbol of femininity, fertility and natural cycles. Lunar cycles serve as timekeepers and trigger specific activities or ceremonies.

Star Clusters and Constellations
Some Native American tribes view stars as ancestral spirits, while others use stellar features in storytelling, as seasonal markers or for navigation.

NATIVE AMERICAN ASTROLOGICAL MYTHS

Hopi Creation Myth

The Hopi people, from the south-west region of the United States, believe in a creation myth that describes their transition from the previous world to the current one. Their storytelling centres around the sun and moon, which symbolize different aspects of life and creation.

Cheyenne Star Legends

The Cheyenne tribe preserves cultural knowledge by passing down star legends, like the tale of Morning Star and Evening Star. These celestial twins, separated by forbidden love, briefly meet at dawn and dusk. The story explains Venus' appearance while imparting cultural values on relationship norms.

Ojibwe Sky Origin Story

The Ojibwe have a creation story where Nanabozho, a cultural hero, travels to the sky realm and retrieves the sun. This myth explains the cycles of day and night and the changing seasons.

★ ANIMAL TOTEMS AND ★ CONSTELLATIONS

The Ojibwe, or Chippewa, have a distinct animal zodiac system that connects people with specific animal totems based on their birth date. These totems represent their personality traits, strengths and challenges.

No fixed, comprehensive or universally standardized zodiac system exists among all Ojibwe communities. The following information is a generalization and may not be consistent across all Ojibwe groups:

**Bear or Makwa
(22 December–
19 January)**
Constellation: Ursa Major
(the Great Bear).
Symbolism: Strength,
introspection and healing.

**Otter or Nigig
(20 January–
18 February)**
Constellation: No
specific constellation.
Symbolism: Playfulness,
joy and curiosity.

**Cougar or Panther
(19 February–
20 March)**
Constellation: Leo
(the Lion).
Symbolism: Leadership,
courage and adaptability.

**Red Hawk or Migizi
(21 March–19 April)**
Constellation: Cygnus (the
Swan) or Aquila (the Eagle).
Symbolism: Vision, spiritual
awareness and protection.

**Beaver or Amik
(20 April–20 May)**
Constellation: Ursa
Minor (the Little Bear).
Symbolism: Creativity,
diligence and building
a foundation.

**Deer or Oji
(21 May–20 June)**
Constellation: Cepheus
(the King).
Symbolism: Gentleness,
sensitivity and intuition.

**Woodpecker or Zagime
(21 June–21 July)**
Constellation: Columba
(the Dove).
Symbolism: Nurturing,
family and protection.

**Salmon or Name
(22 July–21 August)**
Constellation: Delphinus
(the Dolphin).
Symbolism: Determination,
wisdom and transformation.

**Bear Cub or Mkwa'oons
(22 August–21 September)**
Constellation: Ursa Minor
(The Little Bear).
Symbolism: Youthfulness,
curiosity and developing
strength and skills.

**Raven or Gwiingwiishi
(22 September–
22 October)**
Constellation: Corvus
(the Crow).
Symbolism: Change,
adaptability and intelligence.

**Snake or Naag
(23 October–
22 November)**
Constellation: Serpens
(the Serpent).
Symbolism: Transformation,
healing and intuition.

**Elk or Moos
(23 November–
21 December)**
Constellation: Cetus
(the Whale).
Symbolism: Strength,
nobility and agility.

THE HISTORY OF WESTERN ASTROLOGY

Modern Western astrology is akin to a river that traces its course through the vast landscape of human history. Its source lies in the ancient practices of Mesopotamia, Egypt, China and Greece, where early astrological currents merged with astronomy, philosophy and spirituality.

This ancient tributary navigated Mesopotamia, where Babylonian astronomers contributed to the formation of the zodiac. Celestial observations reflected in Egyptian architecture and intricate star knowledge from China added to the flow. Greek philosophers, notably Pythagoras, played a pivotal role in carving the evolving path.

Astrology gained pace in the Hellenistic era when it sailed through the fertile grounds of Greece. Ptolemy's *Tetrabiblos* combined mathematical astronomy with astrological interpretations to establish the 12 zodiac signs, houses and planetary aspects.

Carving a path through medieval Europe, astrology navigated the Roman Empire and the Islamic world, enriched by a current of Christian philosophy.

During the Renaissance, scholars like Marsilio Ficino and Johannes Kepler took to the waters with their study of celestial connections. Kepler was fascinated by the connection between the moon and tides.

Astrology came up against scepticism and scientific rigour in the Age of Enlightenment, yet traditions persisted. Almanacs and astrological publications bubbled up, capturing the imagination of a diverse audience.

In the twentieth century, astrology surged with newfound vigour. Psychological astrology, influenced by Carl Jung, represented a coming together of different tributaries. Astrology transformed and flowed into the mainstream as a tool for self-discovery and personal growth.

In the late twentieth century, astrology branched into diverse streams. Sun-sign astrology became a prominent current, embraced by newspapers, magazines and online platforms. In the vast ocean of New Age spirituality, astrology is riding the waves.

THE FUNDAMENTALS OF WESTERN ASTROLOGY

Western astrology seeks to understand how the positions of celestial bodies influence individuals and events on Earth. Astrologers use birth charts (also called natal charts) or horoscopes to capture a snapshot of the sky at the exact moment and place of a person's birth. By interpreting the interactions between planets, zodiac signs and astrological houses in this chart, they aim to understand an individual's unique qualities and experiences.

Western astrology uses the tropical zodiac, dividing the sun's path into 12 segments associated with different zodiac signs, each representing specific personality traits and characteristics with a ruling planet.

Astrological aspects – the angular relationships between planets – indicate how celestial energies interact in a birth chart, influencing an individual's personality, relationships and life experiences.

Astrologers also use techniques like transits and progressions, examining the ongoing movements of planets within the chart, to provide insights into future developments.

★ WESTERN ASTROLOGY ★ AND PSYCHOLOGY

Carl Jung, a Swiss psychiatrist and psychoanalyst who practised in the mid-twentieth century, is widely considered one of the most influential thinkers in psychology. His theories and ideas significantly impacted various disciplines, including astrology.

Jung believed that the human psyche is shaped not only by individual experiences but also by universal symbols and patterns. In the 1960s and 1970s, astrologers were drawn to these ideas as they sought to imbue astrology with greater psychological depth.

Jung's concepts of archetypes and universal symbols representing fundamental human experiences became integral to understanding planetary and zodiacal symbolism in birth charts. Astrologers also embraced the idea of the collective unconscious, believing that celestial configurations mirrored universal human themes. Astrologers incorporated Jung's concept of individuation – personal growth and self-realization – into their astrological analysis.

★THE IMPORTANCE OF SUN SIGNS IN WESTERN ASTROLOGY★

In Modern Western astrology, your sun sign is your astrological identity, defining your core traits, preferences and patterns of self-expression. It's like the headline of your personal story, highlighting your drive and aspirations.

Unlike the moon and other planets, which change signs relatively quickly, the sun spends about a month in each sign, making it a more consistent influence. Your sun sign is a stable part of who you are.

Historically, the sun has been considered the most important celestial body in many cultures due to its visibility and critical role in sustaining life on Earth. This centrality is reflected in astrology, where the sun sign has a starring role.

Luckily, it's straightforward to determine your sun sign, since it only depends on your birth date and not your time or place of birth. All you need to know is your birthday!

★ HOROSCOPES ★

Who doesn't love checking out their horoscope? Astrologers create horoscopes by analyzing the current positions of celestial bodies and their impact on each sun sign during a specific period. They write horoscopes with archetypal signs in mind, focusing on sweeping trends and themes. Although horoscopes are great for self-reflection and entertainment, their general nature can be overly simplistic.

You can bring more nuance and personalization to your sun sign horoscope by seeing it in context alongside horoscopes for your moon or ascendant signs.

A moon sign horoscope focuses on how the celestial conditions of a specific period affect your emotional landscape and inner self. An ascendant horoscope reveals how your outer self appears in a particular period.

Astrologers can even create horoscopes based on how you will be affected by planetary movements such as Mercury retrograde or Venus transits – concepts we explore in Chapter Three.

Exploring these astrological layers adds depth to your sun sign horoscope for a more holistic take.

CHAPTER THREE:
READING
THE PLANETS

By now, you likely have an understanding of your sun sign, the zodiac sign in which the sun was present during your birth. You might also be aware of your moon sign, the astrological sign that the moon passed through during your birth.

In this chapter, we will also explore your ascendant sign and delve deeper into the influence of the sun, moon and other celestial bodies.

In Western astrology, astrologers see the sun, moon, Mercury, Venus and Mars as personal planets. They believe these planets provide deep insights into our nature. Their positions in our birth chart shape our core identity, emotional landscape and communication style.

Jupiter, Saturn, Uranus, Neptune and Pluto are seen as outer or transpersonal planets. Astrologers believe their impact extends beyond the individual, weaving generational and overarching life themes.

Let's zoom in on these ideas and explore how they influence your character. Get ready to see yourself in 360-degree detail!

★ SUN SIGNS IN THE SPOTLIGHT ★

On page 60, we discussed sun signs and their influence on personality, behaviour and destiny. Let's delve deeper.

Aries
(21 March–19 April)
Symbol: The Ram
Element: Fire
Ruling Planet: Mars
Attributes: Bold, energetic and ambitious. Natural leaders with a pioneering spirit, but can be impulsive, restless and impatient.

Taurus
(20 April–20 May)
Symbol: The Bull
Element: Earth
Ruling Planet: Venus
Attributes: Practical, reliable and sensual. Grounded individuals with a love for comfort and stability. They can be stubborn, slow to make decisions and averse to change.

Gemini
(21 May–20 June)
Symbol: The Twins
Element: Air
Ruling Planet: Mercury
Attributes: Curious, adaptable and communicative. Quick-witted individuals who thrive on variety and social interaction. They can be fickle, difficult to pin down and two-faced.

Cancer
(21 June–22 July)
Symbol: The Crab
Element: Water
Ruling Planet: The Moon
Attributes: Nurturing, intuitive and empathetic. Emotional protectors with a solid connection to home and family. They can be hoarders and have difficulty letting go.

Leo
(23 July–22 August)
Symbol: The Lion
Element: Fire
Ruling Planet: The Sun
Attributes: Charismatic, confident and generous. Natural leaders with a flair for the dramatic. They can be bossy and easily hurt due to their fragile ego.

Virgo
(23 August–22 September)
Symbol: The Virgin
Element: Earth
Ruling Planet: Mercury
Attributes: Detail-oriented, analytical and practical. Perfectionists with a strong sense of duty. They can be critical and uptight.

Libra
(23 September–22 October)
Symbol: The Scales
Element: Air
Ruling Planet: Venus
Attributes: Charming, diplomatic and sociable. Seekers of balance and harmony in relationships and life. They can have unrealistic expectations of people and be indecisive.

Scorpio
(23 October–21 November)
Symbol: The Scorpion
Element: Water
Ruling Planet: Pluto
Attributes: Intense, determined and mysterious. Deep thinkers with a passion for transformation. They can be jealous and defensive.

**Sagittarius
(22 November–
21 December)**
Symbol: The Archer
Element: Fire
Ruling Planet: Jupiter
Attributes: Optimistic,
adventurous and open-
minded. Free spirits with a love
for exploration and learning.
Can be restless and rebellious.

**Capricorn
(22 December–
19 January)**
Symbol: The Goat
Element: Earth
Ruling Planet: Saturn
Attributes: Ambitious,
disciplined and responsible.
Goal-oriented individuals
with a strong work ethic. They
can appear overly serious,
pessimistic and workaholic.

**Aquarius
(20 January–
18 February)**
Symbol: The Water Carrier
Element: Air
Ruling Planet: Uranus
Attributes: Innovative,
independent and
humanitarian. Visionaries
with a focus on progressive
ideas. They can appear
distant and shallow.

**Pisces
(19 February–
20 March)**
Symbol: The Fish
Element: Water
Ruling Planet: Neptune
Attributes: Intuitive,
compassionate and artistic.
Known for their deep
empathy and creativity, but
can be overly emotional
and prone to escapism.

Next, let's consider other celestial influences for a more
comprehensive understanding.

★ THE ASCENDANT SIGN ★

Let's imagine you make friends with Alex at the airport. On first impressions, he's enthusiastic, outgoing and adventurous.

Later, while travelling together, you discover Alex is actually highly disciplined and goal-oriented despite his carefree exterior. He has a strict itinerary and a checklist of must-see places.

You've just witnessed the contrast between Alex's ascendant (Sagittarius) and sun sign (Capricorn).

The ascendant sign is the constellation rising on the eastern horizon at someone's time of birth. This sign represents the side of their personality they're most comfortable projecting. Each zodiac sign takes two hours to rise over the ascendant, with all 12 signs rising in 24 hours.

As you get to know someone, you uncover different layers of their personality. This process begins with their rising or ascendant sign, followed by their sun sign, which represents their core characteristics and then their moon sign, which reflects their emotional centre.

★ YOUR ASCENDANT SIGN ★

To find your ascendant sign, you'll need your birth time, date and place. You can use an ascendant calculator online or have an astrologer create your natal chart which will show your ascendant.

Aries
Aries Rising individuals exude dynamic, spontaneous, assertive energy. They're natural leaders, often initiating new projects with enthusiasm and courage.

Taurus
Taurus Rising individuals radiate a calm, steady aura. Their grounded, reliable and patient demeanour shapes enduring connections.

Gemini
Quick-witted and adaptable, Gemini Rising people thrive in company. Naturally curious and brilliant networkers, they'll talk to anyone.

Cancer
Although reserved initially, Cancer Rising people soon project warmth and sensitivity. They are approachable, nurturing and create a familiar atmosphere.

Leo
Natural leaders, Leo Rising individuals exude confidence and charisma. They enjoy the spotlight and leave a lasting impression.

Virgo
Virgo Rising signs can appear reserved and discerning. Their service-oriented approach makes them helpful.

Libra

Libra Rising individuals exude charm. Diplomatic, well mannered and pleasant, they create harmony and put people at ease.

Scorpio

Magnetic, intense and mysterious, Scorpio Rising individuals strive to protect their true feelings, which are often deep and passionate.

Sagittarius

Sagittarius Rising individuals can have a boisterous enthusiasm. Adventurous, inspiring and open-minded, they see life's challenges as opportunities for growth.

Capricorn

Capricorn Rising signs can seem shy and sensible. They value professionalism and achievement. In challenging situations, they're wise beyond their years.

Aquarius

Eccentric, forward-thinking and unconventional, Aquarius Rising people are natural rebels. They can seem independent but value collective goals.

Pisces

Pisces Rising individuals exude dreamy, empathetic energy. Artistic and welcoming, they're sensitive, compassionate and elusive all at the same time.

★ MOON SIGNS ★

Do your emotions confuse you? Perhaps you're wondering if there's a deeper meaning behind specific patterns. Or maybe your emotional response to a particular situation is leaving you guessing. The answers lie in your moon sign.

The moon travels through each zodiac sign in about two and a half days, completing its cycle through the Earth's ellipse in roughly one month. Your moon sign is determined by the astrological sign the moon was in at your time of birth.

Due to its reflective and changeable nature, the moon rules your innermost feelings, needs and emotional responses, playing a meaningful role in your relationships and overall emotional well-being. Understanding your moon sign can illuminate greater self-awareness and emotional intelligence.

You can find your moon sign online by inputting your birth date into a birth chart calculator. Even if you don't know your time of birth, you may be able to determine your moon sign if the moon did not change sign on your day of birth.

★ YOUR MOON SIGN ★

Aries Moon
Fiery and impulsive, Aries Moon individuals quickly fall in and out of love. Assertiveness and honesty are marked traits. Learning to consider the consequences of their actions will benefit everyone.

Taurus Moon
Moon in Taurus individuals are committed, secure and careful planners who could benefit from more spontaneity and emotional expression.

Gemini Moon
Those with Moon in Gemini rely on logic and experience rather than instincts. They enjoy mental stimulation but may benefit from deeper emotional connections.

Cancer Moon
Moon in Cancer individuals are highly intuitive, sensitive and protective. They prioritize a comfortable home and family connections but could benefit from learning to let go.

Leo Moon
Behold! These warm and big-hearted personalities shine in the spotlight. They could benefit from putting their ego aside to make space for others.

Virgo Moon
Practical and analytical, Virgo Moons express care through actions. Their shyness hides a romantic heart, but overthinking and trying to fix others can be stressful. Cultivating acceptance can help.

Libra Moon

Those with a Libra Moon value harmony and balance above all. Diplomatic and companionable, they could benefit from being more decisive and accepting of confrontation.

Scorpio Moon

Scorpio Moons experience intense and transformative emotions. They delve deep into the subconscious, valuing emotional authenticity. They could work on their tendency towards secrecy and holding grudges.

Sagittarius Moon

Those with their Moon in Sagittarius are optimistic and adventurous. Freedom, emotional expansion and exploration are crucial to avoid restlessness, but they should address their tendency to run from problems.

Capricorn Moon

Capricorn Moon individuals take emotions seriously and rarely shirk responsibility. They prefer to express care through practical means. Opening up more to others is a helpful goal.

Aquarius Moon

Unconventional and open-minded, people with their Moon in Aquarius are keen to make the world a better place but should deepen their emotional attachments for more intimate connections.

Pisces Moon

Pisces Moon individuals are empathetic and imaginative. They navigate emotions with intuition and creativity but must guard against escapism.

★ MERCURY: THE MESSENGER ★

The Roman god Mercury started life as Hermes, the messenger god of Greek mythology. In astrology, Mercury is considered the planet of communication and daily expression. It represents our mind and how we think and speak. Mercury governs our memory and thought processes and indicates whether we are logical or creative. It also indicates whether we enjoy sharing ideas or working independently.

Mercury in the birth chart

If your ascendant sign has Mercury, it will enhance and emphasize the communication and intellectual tendencies of your public persona. The ascendant sign represents the mask we wear in social situations. In this position, Mercury brings a person's social manners to the fore, even if these traits differ from their true self or sun sign.

The placement of Mercury within a specific sun sign intertwines the Mercurial traits of communication and intellect with an individual's essential nature and core identity. It affects their cognitive style, mental processes, learning preferences, expressiveness, creativity and decision-making tendencies.

★ MERCURY IN RETROGRADE ★

Have you ever felt like you can't say anything right? Emails aren't taken in the spirit you intended, or perhaps they go entirely astray. Maybe you're experiencing Mercury in retrograde.

Mercury appears to slow down and then move backwards across the sky three or four times a year. This phenomenon is known as Mercury in retrograde and lasts about three weeks. It's an optical illusion that occurs due to Earth and Mercury's relative positions and speeds in their orbits around the sun, as seen from Earth.

At these times, areas of life governed by Mercury can feel chaotic and disrupted; think technological glitches, communication misunderstandings and delayed travel plans.

However, it's not all bad. Mercury in retrograde also offers us the opportunity for "time out". It's an opportunity to surrender to a slower pace, to reflect rather than project and to work on your mental clarity.

✦ VENUS: THE COMPANION ✦

When you glimpse Venus twinkling in the morning and evening skies, it's easy to understand why the Romans named this planet after their goddess of love and beauty.

As the second planet from the sun, Venus plays a role in romantic and platonic relationships, attraction and desire. It also rules a person's aesthetic sense and artistic expression.

This planet is all about sensuality and indulgence, motivating people to seek pleasurable experiences and enjoy luxury.

Venus in the birth chart

When Venus is in an ascendant position in a birth chart, it impacts the qualities individuals display on first impressions and the first flush of a relationship – think charm, appearance and romantic ideals.

When Venus is in a sun sign, individuals express their love, creativity and sensuality in ways that are consistent with their sun sign. This close alignment makes for genuine and authentic relationships, aesthetic choices and environments.

★ MARS: THE WARRIOR ★

Are you a go-getter or a laid-back peacemaker, happy to go with the flow?

Astrologers link these personality traits with Mars, the fiery warrior planet. The Romans named this red planet after their god of war and its Greek equivalent, Ares. Both cultures believed it embodied courage, assertiveness, aggression and a willingness to confront challenges.

In astrology, Mars influences our inner drive and ability to take the initiative. It's behind our competitive streak and attitude to winning or losing. Our willpower, independence and willingness to stand up for ourselves are all influenced by Mars.

Mars in the birth chart

Mars' placement in an ascendant sign can influence how confident, competitive, assertive and energetic an individual appears on first impression. Mars indicates an individual's style and strategies in response to discontent or obstacles in a sun sign.

As Mars transits through the zodiac, it often causes conflicts and intense situations, but don't worry – these changes ultimately drive personal growth and development.

★ SATURN: THE TASKMASTER ★

Saturn runs a tight ship! This celestial body is associated with discipline, responsibility and structure. It embodies perseverance, hard work and pragmatism and highlights areas where we must work to learn hard but important lessons.

Facing karma isn't always easy. Saturn shines a light on the parts of our lives where we're most likely to face difficulties or feel inadequate. But this challenging planet also bestows the gift of time, teaching us to slow down and embrace strategic thinking and methodical effort. And when we heed Saturn's stern warnings, we're rewarded with a long-lasting and unshakable sense of achievement.

Saturn in the birth chart

Saturn's placement in a birth chart can affect our attitude towards authority, ambition and the pursuit of success. Individuals with Saturn in their ascendant sign can come across as reserved and formal with a sensible air of discipline and maturity. In a sun sign, Saturn instils responsibility, pragmatism and a focus on long-term goals, presenting challenges as opportunities for growth.

✦ THE SATURN RETURN ✦

Saturn takes around 29 years to return to its original position in a person's birth chart. This rite of passage is called a Saturn Return, often heralding a period of reflection and self-discovery. For some, it reveals that we're far from where we want to be. Others find it helps them embrace responsibilities, promotions or opportunities to prove themselves.

Our first Saturn Return, which occurs around ages 28 to 30, marks the transition from youth to adulthood. It often triggers big life decisions as individuals access their direction and goals.

Fortunately, we get a second chance to refine our goals during our second Saturn Return, which takes place between the ages of 56 and 60. This phase appears as we approach our senior years and raises questions about the purpose of life, legacy and personal satisfaction. As a result, some people may make substantial changes in their careers or relationships.

Although Saturn's transits may bring challenges, they are an opportunity to align our life choices with our true purpose.

★ URANUS: THE REBEL ★

Known as the "Awakener" planet, the Greeks named Uranus after their god of the sky, who was overthrown by his son, leading to a significant shift in power dynamics.

A true revolutionary, Uranus represents rebellion, innovation, independence, unconventional thinking, technological advancements and a desire for freedom and originality.

It encourages individuals to embrace their uniqueness and challenge societal norms, leading to cultural revolutions and societal shifts. On the flip side, this natural tendency towards upheaval and impulsivity may lead to instability and alienation.

Uranus in the birth chart

Those with Uranus in their ascendant sign radiate an avant-garde or fashion-forward aura. They're often trendsetters who wow others with their sudden reinventions or unique take on life.

In a natal chart where Uranus aligns with the sun sign, there is a natural inclination towards progressive thinking, activism and innovation. These individuals may be trailblazers, challenging existing structures and pushing for change.

★ PLUTO: THE TRANSFORMER ★

Pluto, a dwarf planet on the outskirts of our solar system, is often likened to the Roman god of the underworld, Hades. It reveals hidden truths and sparks deep change.

Discovered in 1930, Pluto is also deemed a "generational" planet due to its slow movement through the zodiac. While the sun's path through the zodiac goes through all 12 astrological signs each year, Pluto only moves through a fraction of a sign during this time. Pluto entered Aquarius in March 2023, where it will stay for approximately 20 years.

Pluto in the birth chart

Since Pluto transitions so slowly through each zodiac sign its position influences generational themes more than individual ones. However, when it does align with your sun sign, it amplifies your life's purpose. Pluto's influence on the ascendant creates a magnetic aura, leading to intense relationships.

Pluto's position in your birth chart can also reveal your hidden or darker shadows. Face your fears and Pluto will reward you with the tools for healing and growth.

★ NEPTUNE: THE ENCHANTED ★

Are you a believer, a sceptic or even a false prophet? Where you draw the line is up to you, but anything is possible through Neptune's shifting lens.

This enigmatic planet influences belief, disbelief and the mysterious realm of dreams, illusions and spirituality, bestowing a mystical and enchanting influence.

The name "Neptune" comes from Roman mythology, where this god of the sea was named after his role as the brother of Jupiter and Pluto.

Neptune in the birth chart

Neptune's position in a birth chart reveals the fine line between illusion and enlightenment. It uncovers dreams, subconscious longings, romantic illusions, saviours – and tormentors.

Neptune's impact on the ascendant sign can bring a dreamy air of mystery and spiritual attunement. However, this can come across as elusive or create a disconnect from reality.

Neptune's influence on sun signs brings an ethereal and imaginative quality, enhancing sensitivity, empathy and a connection to the spiritual.

★ JUPITER: THE GIANT ★

Everyone needs a Jupiter in their life! This friendly giant is traditionally known as the "Greater Benefic" thanks to its reputation for growth, good fortune and optimism. Astrologers believe Jupiter brings abundance and expands our perspective on life. The planet is also associated with generosity, wisdom and a love for exploration.

Jupiter in the birth chart

In the natal chart, Jupiter's placement indicates areas where one seeks growth and fulfilment. Astrologers link its positive aspects to optimism, enthusiasm and a propensity for risk-taking.

Jupiter in the ascendant sign enhances an individual's outward demeanour with optimism, generosity and a broadened world view, fostering a positive and expansive approach to life.

Jupiter in the sun sign amplifies one's core identity with a generous and optimistic spirit, encouraging a pursuit of growth, abundance and a positive outlook on life. However, an overly pronounced Jupiter influence may lead to excess, overindulgence or unrealistic expectations.

✶ ALL ABOUT NATAL CHARTS ✶

Let's zoom in on natal charts! As you know from Chapter One, a natal chart is a snapshot of what the heavens looked like when someone was born. They are also called birth charts.

Birth charts are tools used in Western and Vedic astrology. Astrologists create this complex map in various styles, depending on their tradition or goal.

Western charts come in several systems: Placidus is the most popular, dividing the sky based on rising times of zodiac degrees. The Koch system is similar but uses different calculations. The Equal House system assigns each house an equal 30-degree slice, starting from the ascendant. Whole Sign Houses align each zodiac sign with an entire house.

Vedic astrology has two main styles: the North Indian chart, which uses a fixed house system with changing planetary positions and the South Indian chart, which places houses in a square layout.

Modern software offers additional chart types, like bi-wheels, for relationship analysis.

Each astrological tradition has its own set of rules, symbolism and methods of interpretation.

★ THE EQUAL HOUSE SYSTEM ★

The Equal House system is a beginner-friendly method due to its straightforward approach. Each of the 12 houses is precisely 30 degrees, simplifying calculations and interpretations. The ascendant marks the first house, making it easy to identify the chart's starting point and understand its influence on personality.

Unlike others, such as Placidus, this system avoids complications that arise at extreme latitudes. It's consistent everywhere, aiding beginners in learning planetary aspects and house meanings without complex maths. Historical usage across cultures adds to its credibility.

The Equal House system allows a focus on the basics – like zodiac signs, planetary meanings and straightforward aspects – before progressing to more intricate systems. It provides a clear, balanced view of the chart, making astrology accessible and approachable to even complete beginners.

★ CREATING A BIRTH CHART ★

To create a birth chart, you need a birthday, a birth time and place of birth. There are many free online services where you can input your details to generate a birth chart. Some popular websites include Astro.com and CafeAstrology.com. There are also software options for purchase or free download. Alternatively, a professional astrologer can create and interpret your chart.

Your birth chart is a natural starting point, but did you know you can draw charts for events, too? Astrologers often look at the planetary conditions operating at the start of wars, the crowning of monarchs and the rise of politicians. You could create charts to analyze important dates too, such as wedding days or even when someone won the lottery!

Reading a chart may seem daunting at first, but with dedication and persistence, you'll get there. Let's look at an example chart to get started on this exciting journey.

★ LOOKING AT AN
★ EXAMPLE BIRTH CHART ★

This is a birth chart using the Equal House system for someone born on 1 May 1969 at 5.55 p.m. in Glasgow, Scotland. You can obtain a chart for any event you want easily online.

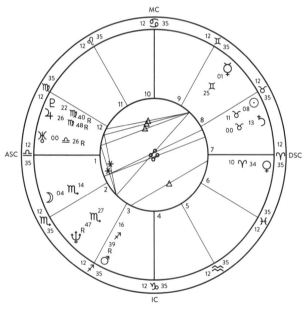

This is the aspectarian grid for the same birth chart, showing the aspects made by each planet and the relevant symbols below.

	☉	☾	☿	♀	♂	♃	♄	♅	♆	♇
☉	☉									
☾	☍	☾								
☿			☿							
♀			△	♀						
♂		△			♂					
♃		☍				♃				
♄			△		☌		♄			
♅								♅		
♆		✳					✳		♆	
♇		△			☌		☌		✳	♇

ASPECTARIAN grid for the birth chart opposite, showing the aspects made by each planet

☌ Conjunction – **0 degrees (strengthening)**

✳ Sextile – **60 degrees apart (harmonious)**

☐ Square – **90 degrees apart (challenging)**

△ Trine – **120 degrees apart (harmonious)**

☍ Opposition – **180 degrees apart (polarizing)**

✦ SYMBOLS KEY ✦

Here's how to interpret the symbols you can see on the chart.

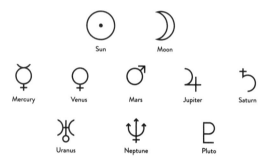

★ READING THE CHART ★

A circular diagram depicts 12 zodiac signs in 30-degree sections, arranged counter-clockwise from the ascendant. Western astrology places the ascendant on the left, representing the chart from the individual's viewpoint. The ascendant marks the cusp of the first house. The other 11 signs complete the circle in a counter-clockwise direction, forming the 12 houses. An empty house in a birth chart indicates there were no planets in that zodiac sign at the time of birth.

The traditional order used to create a narrative in a reading is as follows:

Ascendant
Libra 1st house
associated with Aries

Luminaries
Sun in Taurus (7th house associated with Libra)
Moon in Scorpio (2nd house associated with Taurus)

Inner Planets
Mercury in Gemini (8th house associated with Scorpio)

Venus in Aries (6th house associated with Virgo)
Mars in Sagittarius (3rd house associated with Gemini)

Outer planets
Jupiter in Virgo (12th house associated with Pisces)
Uranus in Libra (12th house associated with Pisces)
Pluto in Virgo (12th house associated with Pisces)

★ INTERPRETING THE NATAL CHART ★

The Taurus **sun** suggests stability, patience and stubbornness, while the Libran seventh house indicates a desire for self-discovery through social interactions.

The **moon** in Scorpio intensifies these traits, creating tension between a need for security and transformative tendencies.

With a Libran **ascendant**, this person seeks to appear pleasant and fair, but emotions may dominate due to the moon in their first house.

Mercury in Gemini boosts mental activity and communication skills, particularly in the eighth house, fostering a desire for deep intellectual connections. The downside of this could be a restless mind.

Venus in Aries signifies an impulsive nature that, while fun, can be inconsistent. Placed in the sixth house, it suggests someone who seeks excitement in their daily routine.

Mars in Sagittarius in the third house reflects an outgoing and broad-minded nature.

Jupiter in Virgo indicates realism and a strong work ethic, though perfectionism may pose challenges, especially in the twelfth house, where imagination and spiritual yearnings emerge.

Saturn in Taurus in the seventh house suggests comfort with older partners, driven by a desire for stability and security.

In Libra, **Uranus** in the twelfth house fosters intuitive psychic connections, potentially leading to vivid dreams and a fascination with the supernatural. Leaving these psychic gifts untapped could lead to frustration.

Neptune in Scorpio enhances imagination or manipulation. In the second house, this could lead to financial deceit or delusion. A positive expression could be a lucrative career in the arts.

Pluto in Virgo drives self-criticism and transformation. The twelfth house turns this inward, fostering a tidy mind. With their introspection in check, this person would make a great therapist.

★ THE PLANETARY ASPECTS ★

The grid on the page opposite the birth chart shows the planetary aspects. The main aspects in this chart are:

★ **Sun opposite Moon:** Sun (core character) polarizing the Moon (emotions).

★ **Moon opposite Saturn:** Moon (emotions) polarizing Saturn (restriction).

★ **Venus trine Mars:** Venus (love/beauty) harmonizes with Mars (desire for action).

★ **Neptune sextile Uranus, Jupiter and Pluto:** Neptune (intuition) harmonizes with Uranus (change), Jupiter (change), Jupiter (luck/expansion) and Pluto (transformation).

★ **Mercury trine Uranus, Jupiter and Pluto:** Mercury (communication) harmonizes with Uranus (change), Jupiter (luck/expansion) and Pluto (transformation).

★ **Neptune opposite Mercury:** Neptune (intuition) opposes Mercury (communication).

★ **Jupiter conjunct Uranus and Pluto:** Jupiter (luck/expansion), Uranus (change) and Pluto (transformation) are all strengthened.

YOUR BIRTH CHART IS JUST THE BEGINNING

Gazing at your birth chart for the first time is like feeling your way in the dark. As your eyes adjust, tiny glimmers of light appear, but where do they lead? What do they mean?

Decoding the planets and their cosmic guidance might seem a world away, but remember, even the most dazzling constellations began with a single star.

This adventure is about the journey, not the destination, where each twinkling insight sparks another question, another wonder.

Enjoy the ride and travel with open eyes and a curious mind. Your birth chart is not a map set in stone. It's a dynamic satnav that illuminates your pathway – pointing out the shortcuts, potholes and beautiful scenery along the way.

The night sky isn't going anywhere and your birth chart is a reminder that you're part of something far bigger than yourself. So whether you're deciphering your chart's every detail or adding depth to your daily horoscope, know that the journey is just beginning. The sky's the limit!

CHAPTER FOUR:
USING ASTROLOGY
IN YOUR LIFE

Congratulations, stargazer! You've soaked up the history of astrology and unlocked the secrets of your birth chart. But what now?

In this final chapter, you'll break free from the history books and dive into hands-on astrological techniques. Here, you'll deepen your connection with astrology in a profoundly personal way.

You'll see how astrology can be a tool for harnessing strengths, harmonizing relationships and understanding personal triggers. Imagine aligning your business venture with lunar cycles, expanding your financial resources during Jupiter's reign, or using Mars' fiery pulse to power your activism.

Prepare to transform your celestial knowledge into a practical superpower. It's time to cast aside your cosmic awe and roll up your sleeves as the next exciting part of your astrological journey unfurls.

ASTROLOGY FOR EMOTIONAL WELL-BEING

Harnessing moon cycles

Astrologers believe the moon significantly influences our emotions and inner self. Your moon sign has a significant role, but did you know tuning into the moon's rhythm can also benefit your emotional well-being?

Like all planets, the moon doesn't make light; it's lit by the sun and the glow we see is a reflection of this light. The sun always lights half the moon, but we see different parts. These changing aspects are known as the moon phases.

Do your emotions sometimes run high during a full moon? Or are you more introspective during the crescent moon phase? Read on to discover how the moon pulls on our emotions during its rhythmical dance around Earth – and how you can harness this powerful energy.

★ The new moon brings a sense of renewal. It's a clean emotional slate and allows you to start afresh. Emotions tend to be introspective, making it an ideal time for setting intentions.

★ During the waxing phase, energy grows and emotions become more outward-facing and driven. The waxing phase amplifies energy, focus and emotional growth.

★ During the full moon, sensitivity and intuition skyrocket. Time to embrace your emotions and feel everything deeply. Expect emotional revelations!

★ In the waning moon phase, energies start to flag and focus lessens. Time to slow down, reflect and release what no longer serves you.

★ FEEL YOUR EMOTIONS TO THEIR ★ FULLEST UNDER A FULL MOON

Every 29.5 days, the moon glides into alignment opposite the Earth, fully reflecting the sun's light and creating the captivating spectacle we know as the full moon. This crescendo is when astrologers believe her energies peak.

You may feel the pull of your moon sign more powerfully now. Balance this by practising these rituals and meditations tailored to your moon sign under a full moon.

Aries moon sign: Sit with your feelings. Just for one night, allow yourself to wallow.

Taurus moon sign: Dance under the moon to release any stuck emotions.

Gemini moon sign: Tune in to your body and step away from your thinking mind.

Cancer moon sign: Take a moonlit bath to wash away anything that no longer serves you.

Leo moon sign: Let the moon take centre stage tonight and enjoy being her audience.

Virgo moon sign: Resist the need to fix things. Put your trust in forces bigger than yourself.

Libra moon sign: Meditate and embrace confrontations or fear of standing alone.

Scorpio moon sign: Visualize the moon's light illuminating hidden vulnerabilities.

Sagittarius moon sign: Stop running from what scares you and find stillness.

Capricorn moon sign: Visualize your emotions as moonbeams, shining on everyone you meet.

Aquarius moon sign: Light a fire and gather friends for a sharing circle.

Pisces moon sign: Take some "me time" to be creative.

★ DIVINE TIMING ★

Did you know you can use astrological conditions to maximize career success? Astrology apps, websites, calendars, almanacs and social media channels often detail current astrological conditions.

★ New moons support new ventures or job offers. Set intentions and make plans.
★ Jupiter's movement increases optimism and opens doors for professional growth; look for times when Jupiter is prominent in the sky.
★ Harmonious aspects between the sun and Jupiter often bring smooth transitions and collaborations.
★ Solar and lunar eclipses shake up the status quo, clearing paths for new professional directions.

Challenging periods for career moves
★ Mercury retrogrades disrupt communication and cause delays. Be patient.
★ Significant movements of Saturn bring challenges. Focus on learning and resilience.
★ Eclipses signify abrupt changes. Remain adaptable but not impulsive.

⋆ ASTROLOGY FOR ⋆ A STELLAR CAREER

When it comes to your career, aim for the stars! The midheaven point, or medium coeli, in your birth chart is the highest point above the horizon at the time of your birth. This point symbolizes your career goals, public image and social status.

So, if you need a career boost or are struggling with a workplace conundrum, look to your midheaven point for inspiration. Or perhaps you're unfulfilled and looking for a new direction. Try leveraging the strengths associated with your midheaven sign and expect stellar results!

You can use online birth chart calculators, or even astrological apps, to identify your midheaven point. Select "whole signs" as the house system and look for the symbol "MC" at the top of the chart. The zodiac sign intersecting that line reveals your midheaven.

★ MIDHEAVEN SIGNS ★

Aries midheaven
Leverage: Your initiative and leadership skills.
Strategy: Make a start and others will
follow – be inspired and inspiring!

Taurus midheaven
Leverage: Your stability and practicality.
Strategy: Focus on long-term goals, reliability and practical
solutions. Your level-headed approach will win out.

Gemini midheaven
Leverage: Your communication and versatility.
Strategy: Ask around and turn your hand to anything that
comes up – at your best, you're an approachable all-rounder.

Cancer midheaven
Leverage: Your nurturing attention to detail.
Strategy: Be the person who notices the little things
that make a big difference – that's your superpower.

Leo midheaven
Leverage: Your confidence and creativity.
Strategy: Let your charisma light up the room and
enthuse others – you make a great team leader!

Virgo midheaven
Leverage: Your analytical and detail-oriented skills.
Strategy: Use your analytical skills to pick up on
details others miss and offer practical solutions.

Libra midheaven
Leverage: Your diplomacy and charm.
Strategy: Foster harmony, find common ground and negotiate mutually beneficial solutions for everyone.

Scorpio midheaven
Leverage: Your intensity and intuition.
Strategy: If you get a hunch, don't be afraid to follow it – with the passion only you can bring.

Sagittarius midheaven
Leverage: Your adventure and optimism.
Strategy: Let your can-do, open-minded attitude find growth in all situations.

Capricorn midheaven
Leverage: Your ambition and discipline.
Strategy: Aim high, create a plan and set your mind to it. Nothing beats Capricorn's commitment!

Aquarius midheaven
Leverage: Your innovation and independence.
Strategy: Capitalize on your inimitable perspective and vision – it's your unique selling point!

Pisces midheaven
Leverage: Your compassion and creativity.
Strategy: Let your intuition guide you towards creative collaborations – you'll create something extraordinary!

RELATIONSHIPS
★ WRITTEN IN THE STARS ★

How long does it take you to start sizing up zodiac traits in potential partners?

Astrology offers a powerful lens to explore the natural chemistry between two souls. The practice of synastry or composite charts allows us to zoom in on unique areas of attraction and affinity in a partnership. But you can still get a feel for compatibility without birth chart information.

Knowing someone's sun sign can give us a sense of how we may interact with them. Some pairings crackle and spark, igniting passion. Some mirror each other, offering easy reflection. Others stretch us due to their polar position in the zodiac.

Astrology isn't about predicting a relationship's destiny but shining a light on areas of connection, harmony and transformative possibility. It can help us navigate patterns, clashes and synergies. So, embrace your astrological dance with another, but remember – the stars may whisper a melody, but you are always free to dance to your own tune.

✦ THE COSMIC COCKTAIL PARTY ✦

Imagine throwing a star-studded party to introduce the 12 zodiac signs. Who'd avoid each other? Who'd be having a dance-off? Who'd be whispering in a shadowy corner? It's all down to triplicities, quadruplicities and polarities.

✦ TRIPLICITIES ✦

Each sign belongs to a cosmic clan – fire, air, earth, or water.

Fire signs: Aries, Leo and Sagittarius bring the heat and get the party started.

Air signs: Gemini, Libra and Aquarius are the social butterflies.

Air adores fire's warmth and adventurousness. Fire loves air's intellect and breezy ability to fan their flames.

Earth signs: Taurus, Virgo and Capricorn are considerate guests, helping the party flow.

Water signs: Cancer, Scorpio and Pisces add depth and mystery, getting emotions swirling.

Earth finds solace in water's emotional intelligence, while water welcomes earth's stability.

★ QUADRUPLICITIES ★

Triplicities are just the beginning – the zodiac cocktail party is also divided into three groups of four signs that share the same qualities. These quadruplicates are named cardinal, fixed and mutable and are grouped as follows:

Cardinal signs:
Aries, Cancer, Libra and Capricorn are the initiators, the mixologists who write the cocktail recipes.

Fixed Signs:
Taurus, Leo, Scorpio and Aquarius are the staple ingredients and trusted favourites that no party is complete without.

Mutable signs:
Gemini, Virgo, Sagittarius and Pisces are the creative flourishes and innovative blends inspired by the evening.

The flavours don't always come together – **cardinals** might grow bored by **fixed** signs and **mutables** may clash with **fixed** signs. But when they find harmony, these diverse ingredients complement each other in delicious flavour sensations.

★ POLARITIES ★

Have you ever wondered why opposites attract but drive each other crazy at the same time? Astrologers often explain this through polarities. The zodiac has six pairs of opposing signs with complementary and contrasting energies. The polarities are:

★ **Aries (Fire) v. Libra (Air):** independence v. compromise, action v. diplomacy, impulsivity v. balance

★ **Taurus (Earth) v. Scorpio (Water):** practicality v. passion, sensuality v. security, possessiveness v. abundance

★ **Gemini (Air) v. Sagittarius (Fire):** curiosity v. conviction, playfulness v. purpose, scattering ideas v. chasing goals

★ **Cancer (Water) v. Capricorn (Earth):** nurturing v. building, emotional security v. material stability, inner exploration v. external accomplishment

★ **Leo (Fire) v. Aquarius (Air):** creativity v. innovation, self-expression v. humanitarian vision, attention-seeking v. altruistic

★ **Virgo (Earth) v. Pisces (Water):** analysis v. empathy, service v. intuition, groundedness v. mysticism

★ ASTROLOGY FOR SPIRITUALITY ★

Do you ever gaze at the stars and feel a sense of wonder? A desire to connect with the universe and understand your place in it? Astrology is not just a fortune-teller's game but a shimmering bridge between you and the heavens.

For thousands of years, stargazers have woven the movements of planets and stars into their spiritual practices and beliefs. The rhythms of the universe have inspired rituals, myths and even the stories of our gods, fostering a sense of belonging to something greater than ourselves. Astrology reminds us that we are part of a larger cosmic story that spans all religions and cultures, that has been unfolding for aeons and will continue to do so long after we're gone.

How you incorporate astrology into your spiritual journey is deeply personal; it doesn't impose dogmas or challenge existing beliefs but can complement your practices, adding depth and unique meaning to your connection with the divine.

★ ASTROLOGICAL RITUALS TO ★ DEEPEN YOUR SPIRITUALITY

Renew spiritual connections under the new moon

Sit under a new moon. Purify yourself with burning herbs or incense. Light a new candle and invite your preferred divine energy into the space. Silently bathe in the new moon's beams. Purify doubts and feel a renewed connection.

Channel the divine through celestial bodies

Contemplate the night sky and any visible celestial bodies. See them as divine manifestations or representations of deities from your tradition. Do they carry any messages to help strengthen your spirituality? Note any insights in a journal. Make a symbolic offering to deepen your connection and show gratitude. Close with a moment of stillness, kindling reverence and appreciation.

Evoke Saturn to build a spiritual routine

Get up at sunrise to witness Saturn's appearance in the sky. Hold a crystal, light a candle and chant a mantra to connect with the divine. Ask Saturn to help you stick to any spiritual routines throughout the day. Carry the charged crystal as a reminder of your commitments.

★ DIVINE INSPIRATION OF ★ ASTROLOGICAL EVENTS

Throughout history, many cultures have linked astronomical events to sacred moments.

Sunrises and sunsets: The Hopi tribe's elders chant sunrise prayers to express appreciation and promote well-being. At Shinto shrines, priests conduct rituals facing the rising sun, which they see as a source of life and renewal.

Solstices: The winter solstice is the shortest day, with celebrations like pagan Yule and Yalda in Iran. The summer solstice is the longest day, with festivals like Midsummer in Scandinavia and Ivan Kupala in Russia and Ukraine.

Solar eclipses: In ancient Chinese and Mayan cultures, drumming and chanting protected the sun during eclipses. Today, modern pagans reflect and release negativity during eclipses.

Full moons: Full moons have been linked to increased energy and intensified emotions. Hindus celebrate "Raksha Bandhan" to strengthen sibling bonds, while

Native American tribes perform cleansing rituals, releasing negativity.

New moons: New moons symbolize new beginnings and are perfect for setting intentions. Wiccan celebrations like Samhain and Ostara occur on new moons, focusing on themes of death and rebirth, spring and renewal.

Lunar eclipses: Rituals in Hindu and Buddhist traditions often include meditation and chanting to appease celestial wrath. Some modern practices view eclipses as times for deep inner work.

Meteor showers: Shooting stars are often associated with making wishes and reflecting on hopes and dreams. In Japan, they fire flaming arrows into the sky during the Perseid meteor shower, symbolizing wishes and cleansing misfortune.

Explore astrological traditions and rituals that resonate with your beliefs and spiritual inclinations. Some astrological practices involve cultural symbols or customs: make sure you understand and respect their cultural context before using them.

★ ASTROLOGY FOR ★ FINANCIAL FREEDOM

Ready to transform your relationship with money, one star-studded step at a time? Read on to discover a cosmic treasure map leading you towards abundance and healthy financial habits.

As the planet of expansion, luck, optimism and prosperity, Jupiter is all about exponential growth. Channel this expansive energy to attract abundance into your life next time Jupiter is in a favourable position for financial matters. This time could be when:

★ Jupiter changes from retrograde to direct motion.
★ Jupiter moves into a new sign.
★ Jupiter is in a favourable aspect with a new moon.
★ Jupiter is in a harmonious aspect with Venus.
★ It is your Jupiter Return – around the ages of 12, 24, 36, 48, 60, 72, 84 and 96.

During this period, consciously donate to a cause you feel passionate about or surprise someone with a small anonymous gift. Visualize the act creating a ripple of generosity, bringing prosperity back to you.

TAKE CONTROL OF YOUR
✦ FINANCIAL OBLIGATIONS ✦
WITH PLANETARY POWER

Are you worried about repaying your debts? Or perhaps you've been burying your head in the sand and need to take more financial responsibility. Look no further than the sixth planet from the sun: Saturn.

Astrologers link the rings of Saturn to financial responsibility and the principle of reaping what you sow. Saturn is the planet of discipline and structure, while his rings symbolize the cyclical nature of financial obligations. Try this meditation to tap into Saturn's support.

Draw a circle on a soft surface like a sandy beach or woodland floor. Place a black rock in the centre, symbolizing Saturn. Step into the circle beside the rock. You've now entered Saturn's realm. Feel his grounding energy and rings encircling you, swirling away your worries. Repeat affirmations declaring your control over financial matters. Express gratitude to Saturn for his support. Step away, knowing Saturn has your back. Visualizing this exercise is just as powerful as doing it in reality.

★ CULTIVATE WISE SPENDING WITH ASTRO-HABITS ★

Venus is known as the planet of beauty and quality, while Mercury is the planet of utility and sensible choices. The next time you feel the urge to make a significant purchase, try tapping into their power.

Choose a clear night under a waxing moon when Venus and Mercury are visible. Take two distinct coins outside and hold them in your hands. Face south-west; inhale Venus' energy of pleasure and luxury. Ask her how to spend money for lasting joy. Consider if the purchase will bring lasting beauty and enjoyment. Next, turn to the north-west and feel Mercury's clarity and discernment. Analyze the purchase; is it something you genuinely need, or a fleeting want? Can you afford it without causing stress? Thank the planets for their wisdom and ask them to guide your purchasing decisions in future.

Carry the coins in an accessible pocket and refer to them whenever you want to buy something. This practice will help you make more thoughtful and mindful purchases.

UNLEASH YOUR FINANCIAL POWER WITH COSMIC GUIDANCE

Your natal chart holds the blueprint of your relationship with money. The second house, governing personal resources and aspects involving financial planets, like Jupiter (abundance) and Venus (value), whisper clues about your earning potential, spending habits and beliefs that might be holding you back.

To discover your financial blueprint, try exploring your second house. The ruling planet signifies your earning potential, values and financial priorities. Look for planetary interactions that may have positive or negative influences. Tracking the movement of financial planets in your chart can also be revealing – the transits and progressions of Jupiter and Venus reveal opportunities or challenges on your financial landscape.

How has your astrological blueprint manifested in your financial history and expectations?

Under the magic of a new moon, pour your affirmations into a heartfelt letter to your future financially empowered self. Read it aloud into a mirror, sealing your commitment to a new money story.

⋆ ASTROLOGY FOR HEALTH ⋆

Did you know that each zodiac sign is associated with a specific body area and health profile? Understanding these correspondences can help you make lifestyle choices that benefit your astrological sign and enhance holistic well-being. It can help to think of each sign in terms of the nicknames given, as well as their corresponding body parts.

Aries, the "Energetic Initiator"
Key Body Areas: Head and face.
Holistic Health Approach:

★ Channel dynamic energy through vigorous physical activities.
★ Try an Indian head massage to manage head and neck tension.
★ Prioritize a balanced diet to sustain high energy levels.

Taurus, the "Grounded Nourisher"
Key Body Areas: Neck and throat.
Holistic Health Approach:

★ Focus on neck exercises and maintain good posture.
★ Embrace calming activities like meditation for emotional well-being.
★ Adopt a balanced and nutrient-rich diet for overall health.

Gemini, the "Versatile Communicator"
Key Body Areas: Arms, shoulders and hands.
Holistic Health Approach:

★ Keep your hands busy with crafting or playing a musical instrument.
★ Join a book group, play strategy games or learn a language; anything to busy your mind.
★ Latin or ballroom dancing will tap into your social skills and versatility, while giving your arms a workout.

Cancer, the "Nurturing Empath"
Key Body Areas: Chest and stomach.
Holistic Health Approach:

★ Build long-term relationships with therapists, coaches or trainers.
★ Prioritize a diet that supports digestive health.
★ Create a cozy and comforting home space.

Leo, the "Creative Leader"
Key Body Areas: Heart and upper back.
Holistic Health Approach:

★ Support heart health with cardiovascular exercise.
★ Pour your heart out through creative activities.
★ Try heart-opening exercises to build strength in the upper back.

Virgo, the "Analytical Healer"

Key Body Areas: Digestive system and lower abdomen.
Holistic Health Approach:

★ Prioritize gut health with a balanced and mindful diet.
★ Try deep abdominal breath work for stress relief.
★ Create healthy habits that bring a sense of structure.

Libra, the "Harmonious Diplomat"

Key Body Areas: Kidneys and lower back.
Holistic Health Approach:

★ Show your kidneys some love with a balanced diet and lots of hydration.
★ Choose mind–body exercises like yoga to find equilibrium.
★ Embrace holistic beauty and self-care rituals.

Scorpio, the "Transformative Investigator"

Key Body Areas: Reproductive organs and pelvis.
Holistic Health Approach:

★ Stay on top of your reproductive health with regular check-ups.
★ Bottling up your emotions is a no-no: journal, yell into a pillow or try laughter yoga!
★ Prioritize exercises that strengthen the pelvic area.

Sagittarius, the "Adventurous Optimist"

Key Body Areas: Hips and thighs.
Holistic Health Approach:

★ Try climbing or walking to power up the hips and thighs.
★ Stay optimistic with lots of adventure.
★ Make stretching a part of your everyday routine.

Capricorn, the "Disciplined Achiever"
Key Body Areas: Bones, joints and knees.
Holistic Health Approach:

- ★ Prioritize bone health through a diet rich in calcium and vitamin D.
- ★ Maintain a healthy weight to avoid putting pressure on your joints.
- ★ Keep a healthy work-life balance and schedule regular breaks.

Aquarius, the "Innovative Humanitarian"
Key Body Areas: Circulatory system and ankles.
Holistic Health Approach:

- ★ Don't skip the cardio for circulatory health.
- ★ Seek out activities that align with humanitarian values.
- ★ Try mindful walking, but be sure to wear supportive footwear.

Pisces, the "Intuitive Dreamer"
Key Body Areas: Feet and the lymphatic system.
Holistic Health Approach:

- ★ Invest in comfortable footwear, regular pedicures and podiatry.
- ★ Support the lymphatic system with dry brushing, massage and hydration.
- ★ Your intuition, creativity and emotional well-being are interconnected; so tend to all three.

✦ ASTROLOGY FOR THE HOME ✦

Elevate your living spaces with astrological touches that resonate with your zodiac sign.

Aries, Leo and Sagittarius

Fire signs revel in warm, vibrant colours, bold artwork and statement furniture. Metallic elements add glamour and reflect your fiery essence. Enhance the vibe with fiery pieces, such as candles or log burners.

Taurus, Virgo and Capricorn

Cosy and nature-inspired spaces nurture earth signs. Seek out earthy tones and grounding elements like houseplants or crystals. Antique or handcrafted items will bring a timeless feel. Natural materials like wood, wool or linen are your friends.

Gemini, Libra and Aquarius

Air signs appreciate open modern spaces with light hues and intellectual curiosities like books or art. A minimalist approach helps your productivity, but remember to nurture creativity with unique art installations.

Cancer, Scorpio and Pisces

Water signs find serenity in soothing colours and soft textures. Source flowing fabrics and water features but add emotional depth with family photos or sentimental artefacts.

Follow your intuition; creating a balanced environment that channels all elemental energies can also be grounding.

⋆ ASTROLOGICAL AFFIRMATIONS ⋆

Who doesn't need an occasional pick-me-up? Affirmations can create an instant mood boost, but writing them doesn't always come easily. That's where these ready-made affirmations come in. Tailored to your astrological profile, they go straight to the heart of your best self. Follow these suggestions or use them as inspiration – and feel your spirit soar!

Aries

Chant these affirmations as you dance, walk or run, or scratch them into a candle and burn it.

★ "I am the creator of my own path."
★ "My energy is a force for positive change."
★ "I embrace challenges with courage and resilience."

Taurus

Scratch these affirmations into sand or clay or incorporate them into an altar at home.

★ "I am grounded, stable and secure."
★ "I attract abundance into my life effortlessly."
★ "Patience and persistence lead me to success."

Gemini

Speak these affirmations into a mirror or tell a trusted friend.

★ "My mind is sharp and my thoughts are clear."
★ "I embrace change and adapt with ease."
★ "Communication is my superpower, connecting me with others."

Cancer

Make these into wall art for your home or create a family affirmations jar to share.

★ "I am surrounded by love and emotional balance."
★ "I release what no longer serves me with compassion."
★ "My intuition guides me to make wise decisions."

Leo

Incorporate these into a song and sing it to yourself or an audience.

★ "I am confident, radiant and filled with joy."
★ "My creativity knows no bounds."
★ "I shine my light, inspiring others to do the same."

Virgo

These affirmations can go into a journal, or recite them while meditating.

★ "I am organized, focused and in control."

★ "Every detail of my life aligns for my highest good."

★ "I trust in the process of life's perfection."

Libra

Create an aesthetic affirmation collage or include these in a love letter to yourself.

★ "I am in harmony with the world around me."

★ "Balance and beauty flow into every aspect of my life."

★ "My relationships are filled with love and understanding."

Scorpio

Transform these affirmations into poetry or prose, or write them on paper and burn them.

★ "I embrace transformation and let go of the past."

★ "My inner strength guides me through challenges."

★ "I am a powerful creator of my own reality."

Sagittarius

Shout these affirmations from a hilltop or tall building or create a vision board.

★ "Adventure and optimism fuel my journey."
★ "I am open to new possibilities and opportunities."
★ "My spirit is free and my possibilities are limitless."

Capricorn

Incorporate these affirmations into your journal writing, or bury them in the earth.

★ "I am disciplined, focused and determined."
★ "Success is my natural state of being."
★ "I build my foundation for lasting achievements."

Aquarius

Send these affirmations to yourself by email or text message or share them on social media.

★ "I embrace my uniqueness and celebrate diversity."
★ "My innovative ideas create positive change."
★ "I am a beacon of light, inspiring collective progress."

Pisces

Find art that symbolizes these affirmations or repeat them in the bath.

★ "I trust in the flow of life and surrender to the universe."
★ "My creativity and intuition guide me to fulfilment."
★ "Love and compassion are the essence of my being."

★ CONCLUSION: WE ARE ★ ALL MADE OF STARS

What made you pick up this book? Where does your calling for astrology come from? The answer could lie in your cosmic heritage.

In the beginning, the universe was a swirling cocktail of particles. Over billions of years, they united to create stars and forge heavier elements like oxygen, carbon and nitrogen. When these stars exploded into supernovas, they scattered stardust all over the cosmos. In our corner of the universe, this stardust condensed and cooled to form Earth and the building blocks of life. From the calcium in our bones to the iron in our blood, every atom in our bodies is made of stardust.

This remarkable truth explains our instincts to look up, seek truth and take inspiration from the cosmos. Astrology is a powerful way to follow this calling and this book can be your guide – a North Star or Southern Cross.

But you must also remember to follow the yearnings of your heart and soul – because they're made of stars, too.

The Little Book of the Zodiac:
An Introduction to Astrology

Marion Williamson

Paperback
ISBN: 978-1-78685-546-6

Embark on a voyage of self-discovery with this spellbinding introduction to astrology. Learn ways to interpret your birth chart and how your star sign can tell you about your character traits. Let this book shine a light on your past, present and future, and reveal a deeper understanding of your celestial outlook.

The Little Book of Cosmic Energy: A Beginner's Guide to Harnessing the Power of the Universe

Lydia Levine

Paperback
ISBN: 978-1-83799-309-3

Everything, including you, is made up of vibrational energy. By tuning in to a higher frequency and raising your vibration, you can start leading a happier, more purposeful life. This pocket-sized book will be your go-to guide to unlocking the positive energy that surrounds us. It's time to start tapping into the awesome power of the universe.

Have you enjoyed this book? If so, find us
on Facebook at **Summersdale Publishers**,
on Twitter/X at **@Summersdale** and on Instagram
and TikTok at **@summersdalebooks** and get
in touch. We'd love to hear from you!

www.summersdale.com

IMAGE CREDITS